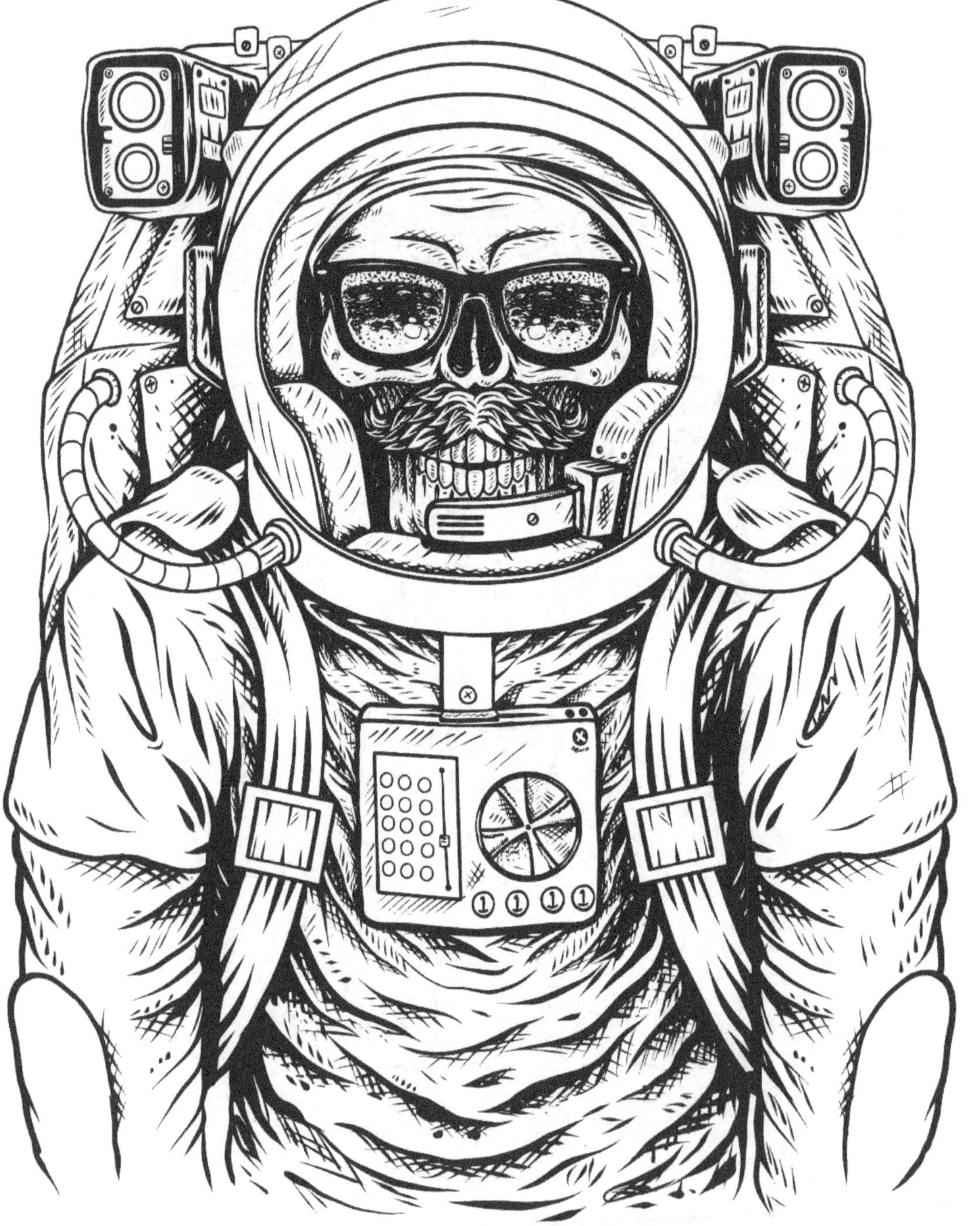

13

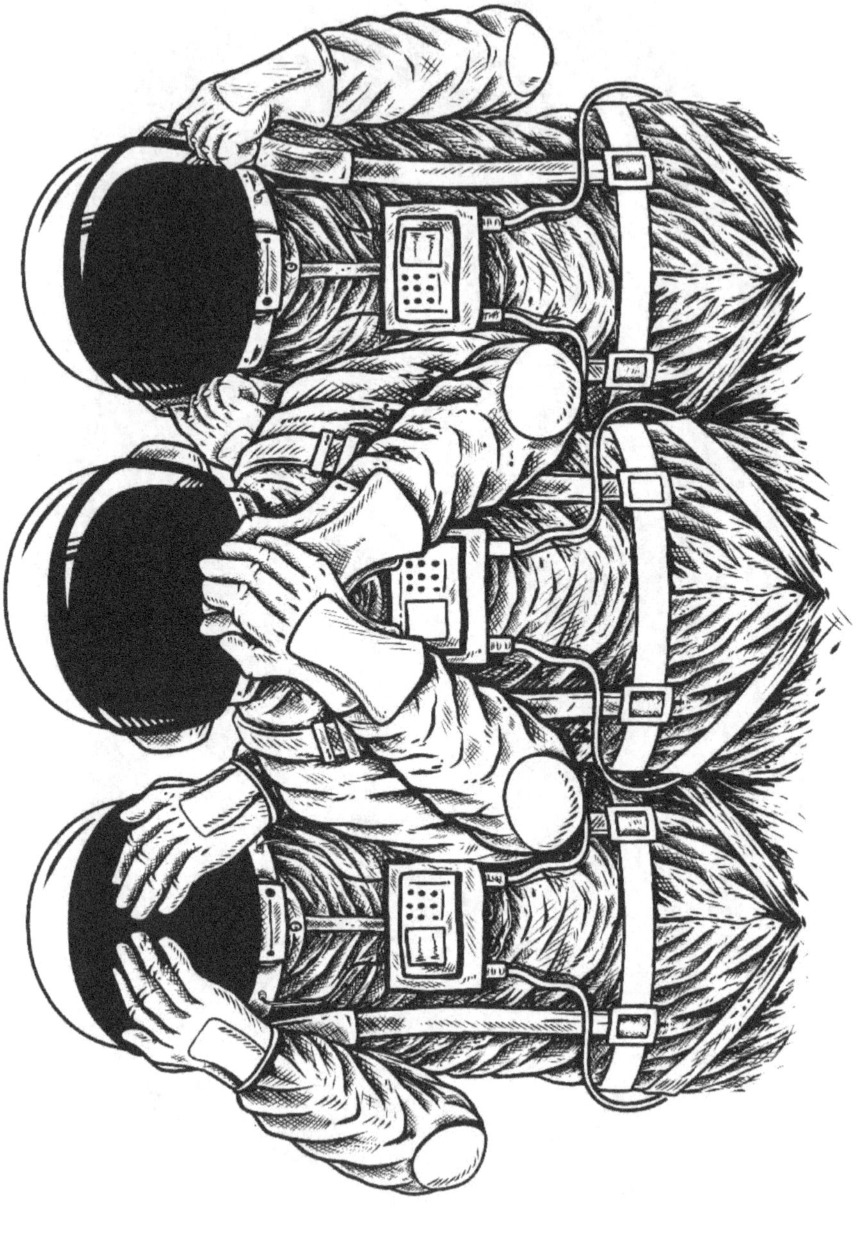

MARS
EARTH
VENUS
JUPITER
MERCURY
SUN
NEPTUNE
URANUS
SATURN

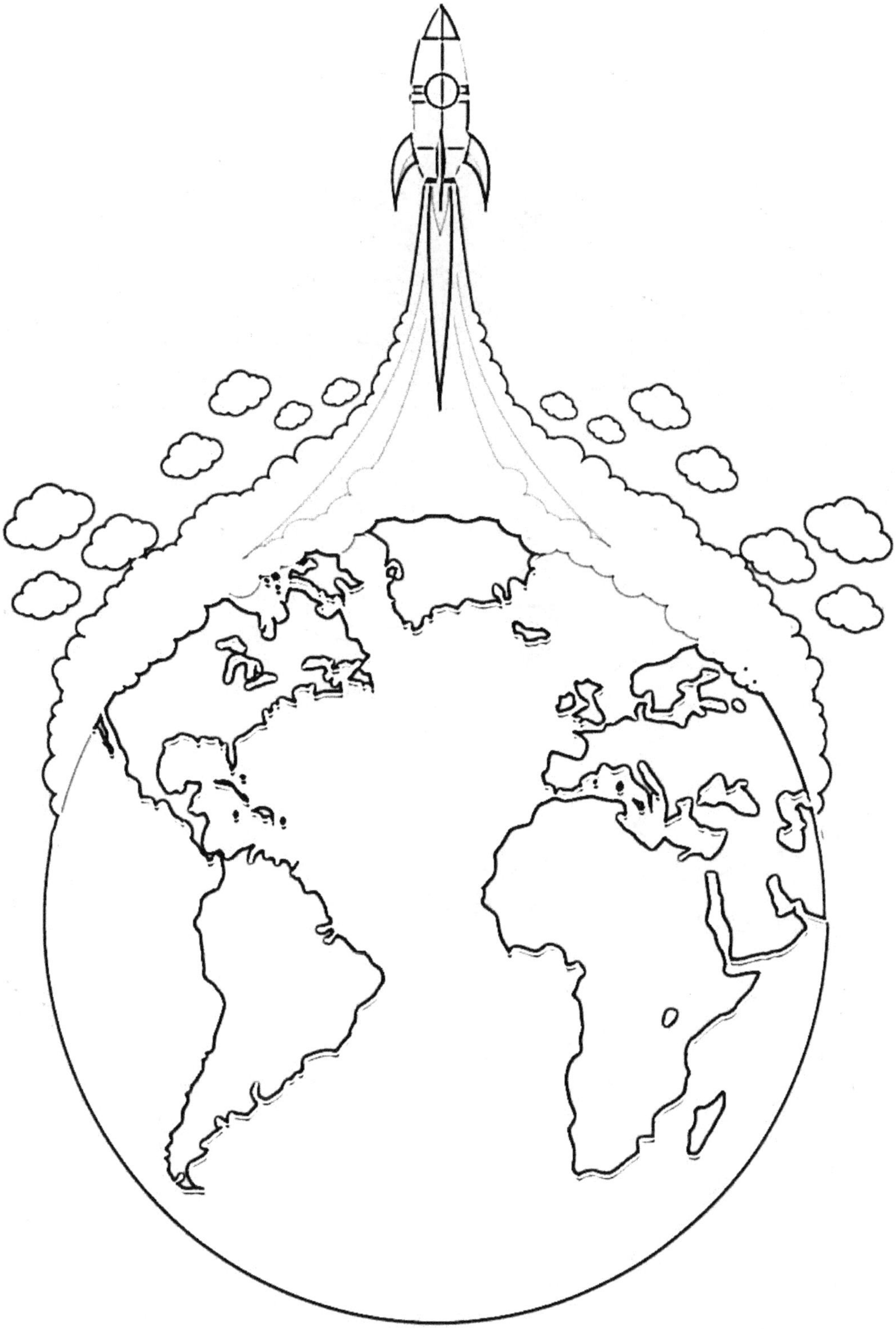

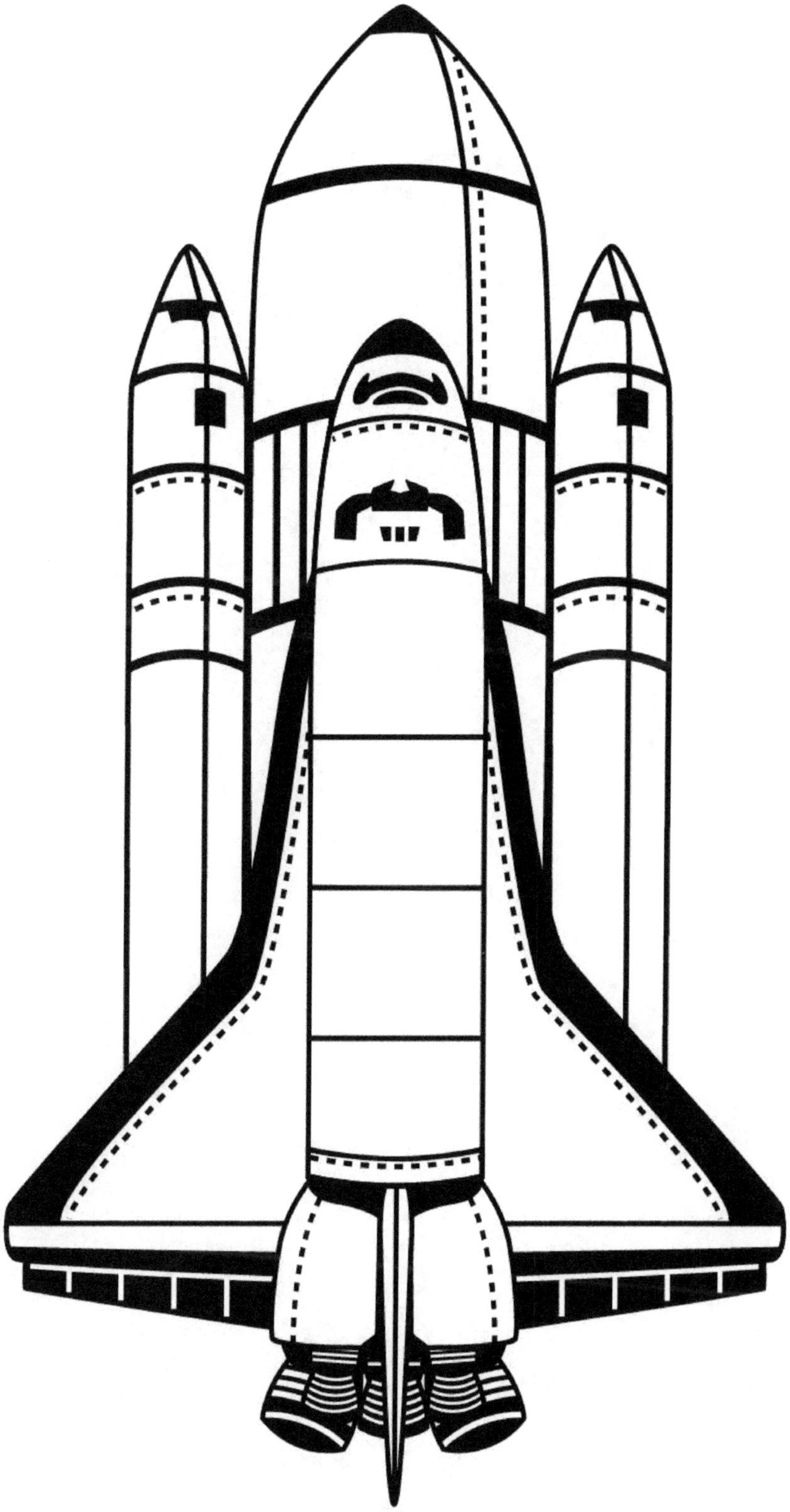

MERCURY
VENUS
EARTH
MARS
JUPITER
SATURN
URANUS
NEPTUNE
PLUTO

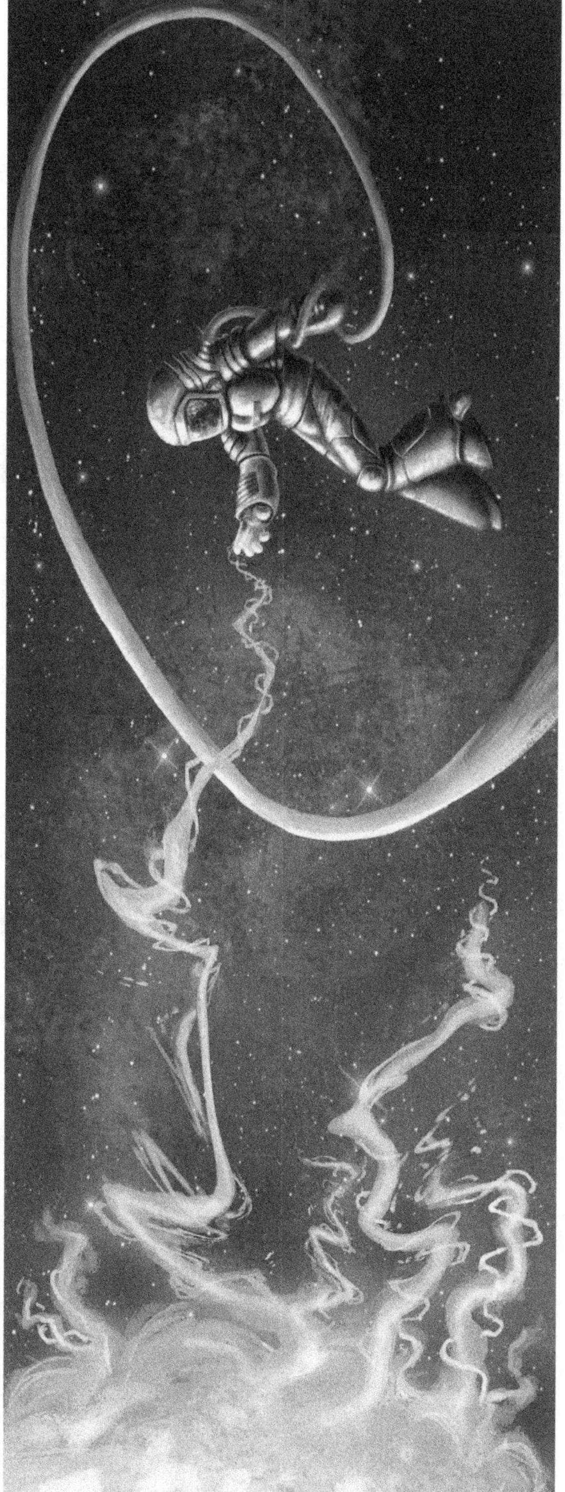

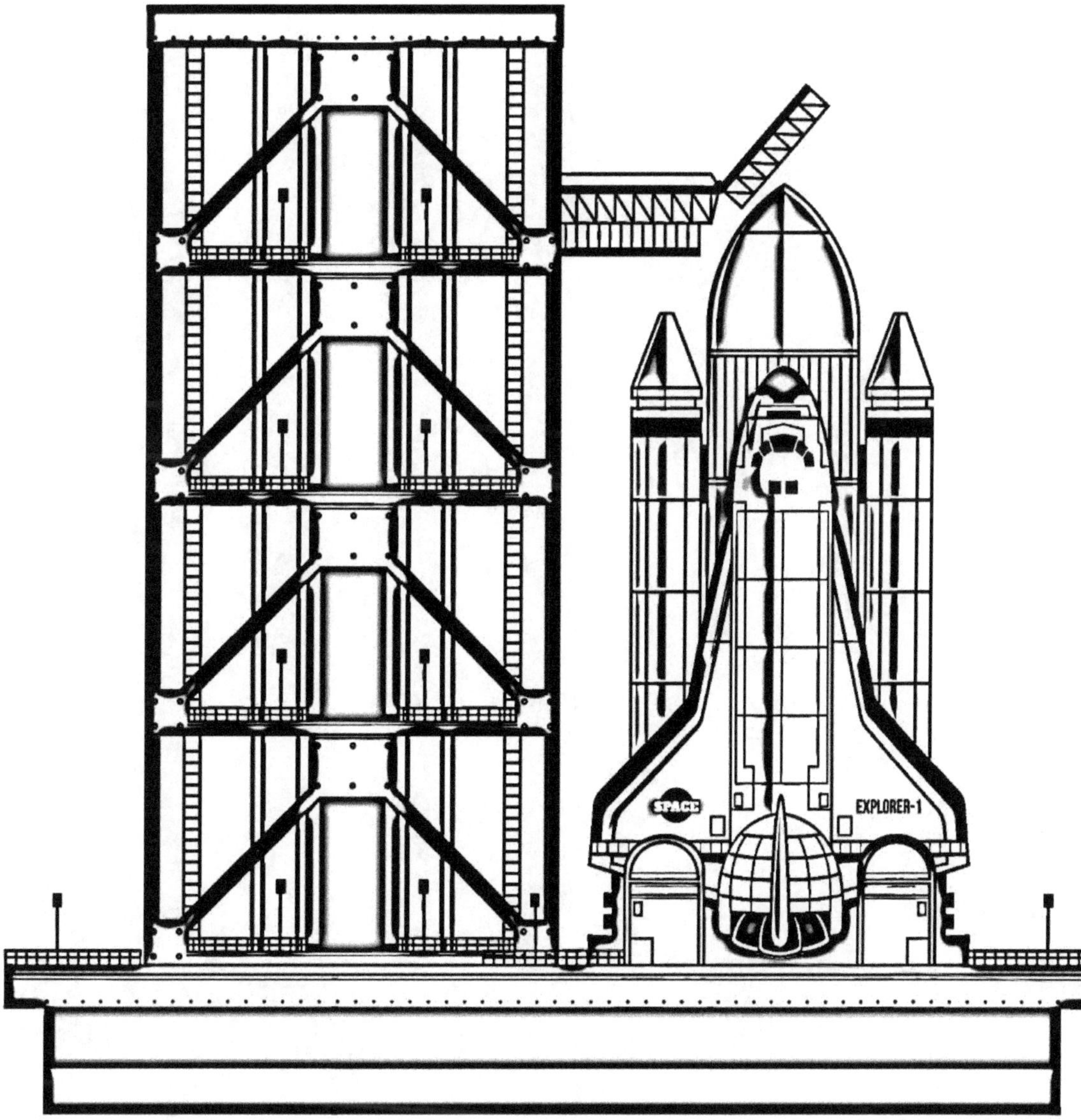
SPACE
EXPLORER-1

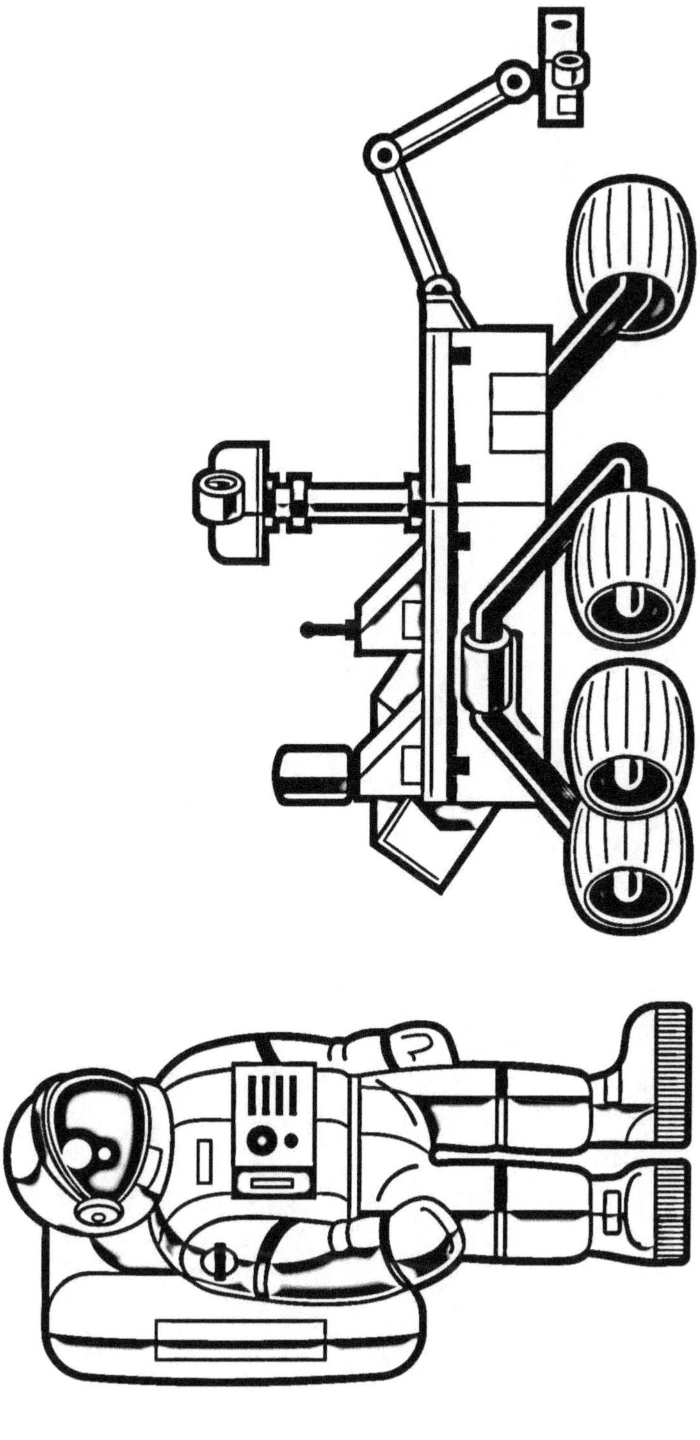

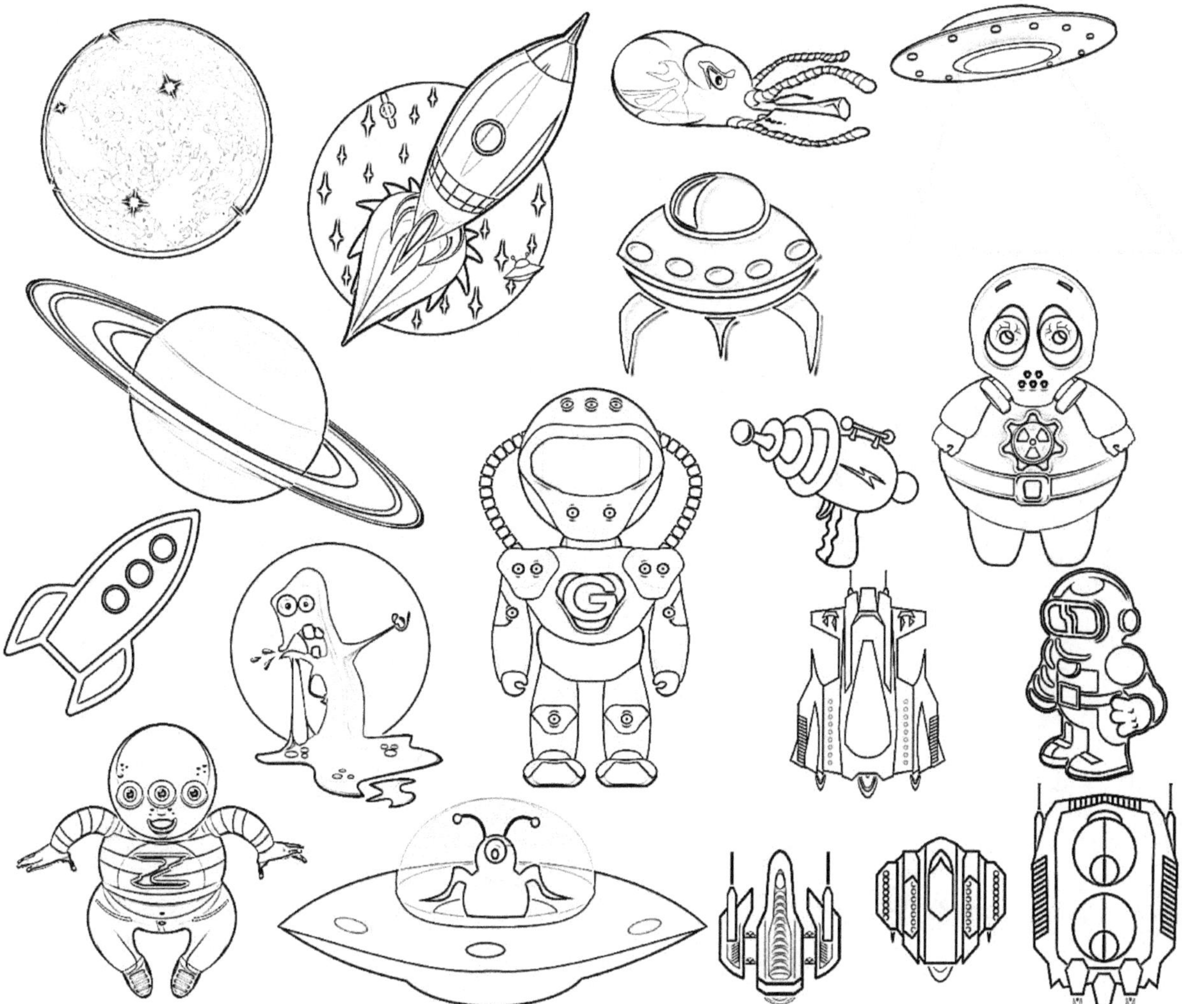

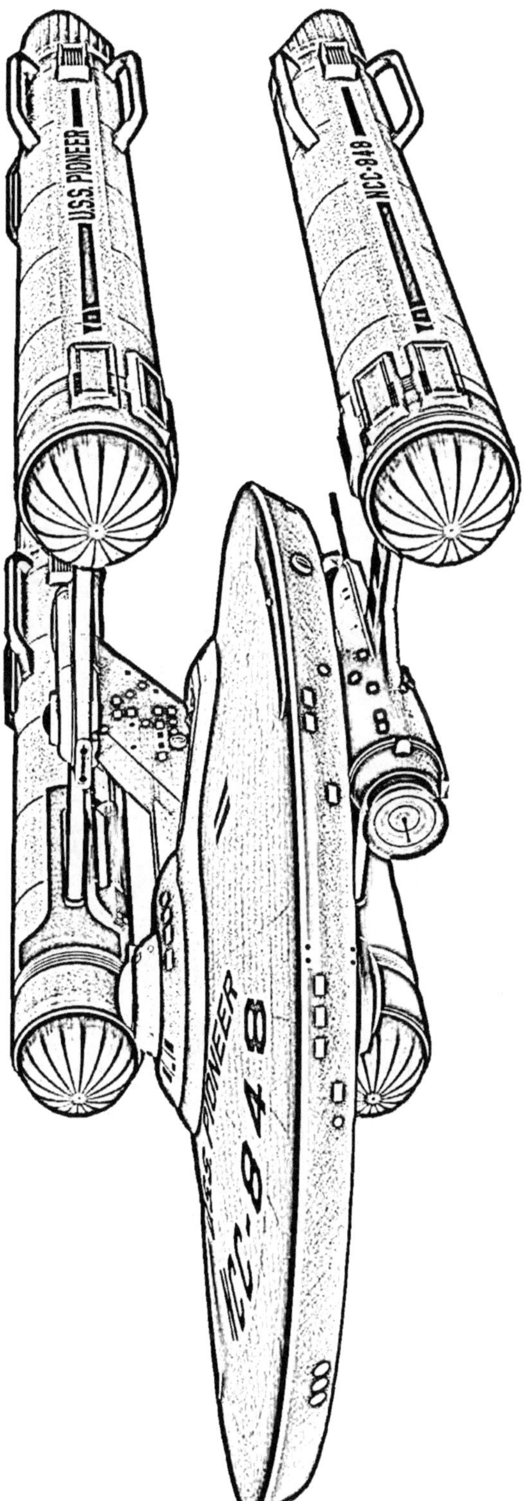
U.S.S. PIONEER
NCC-948

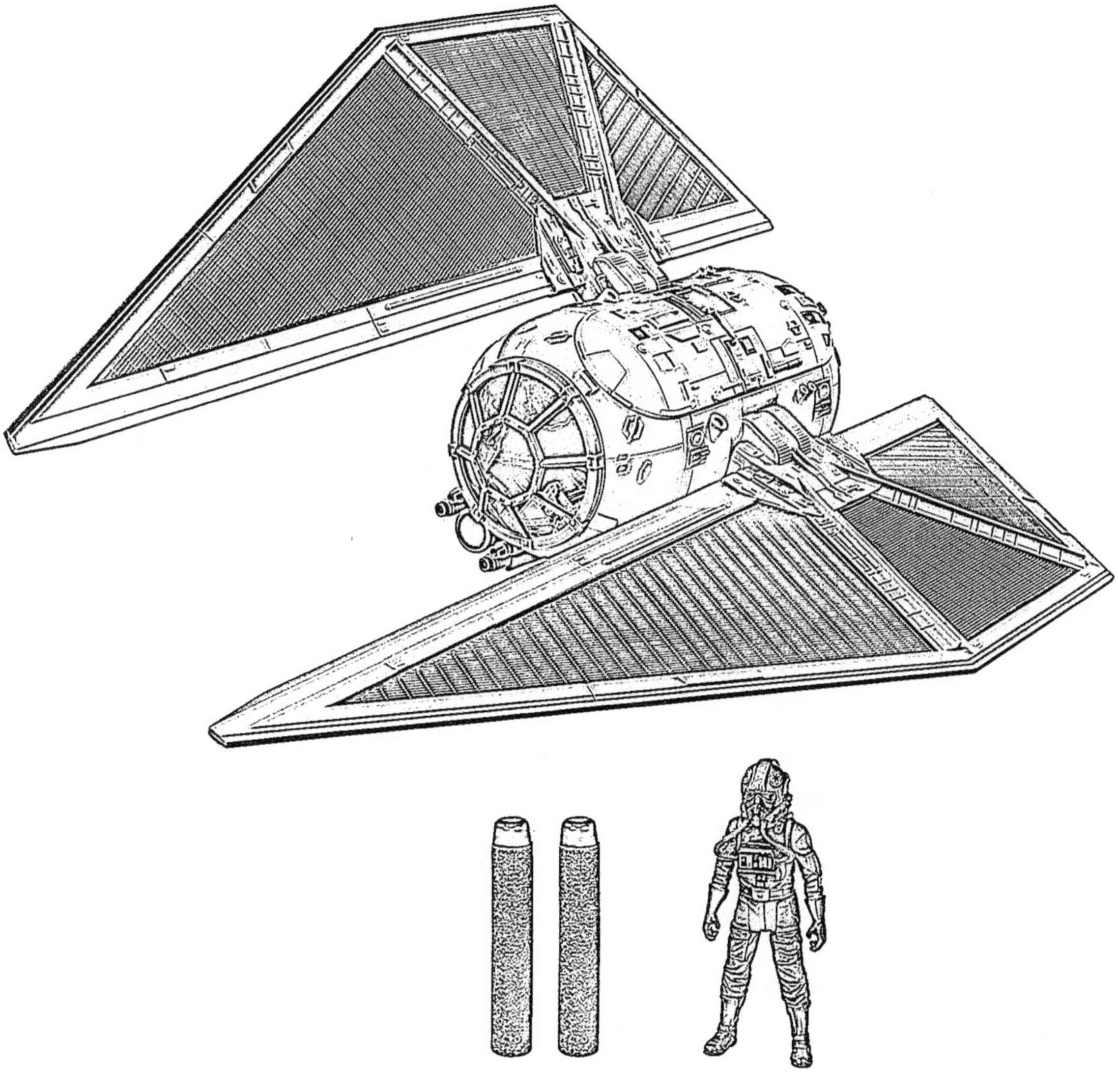

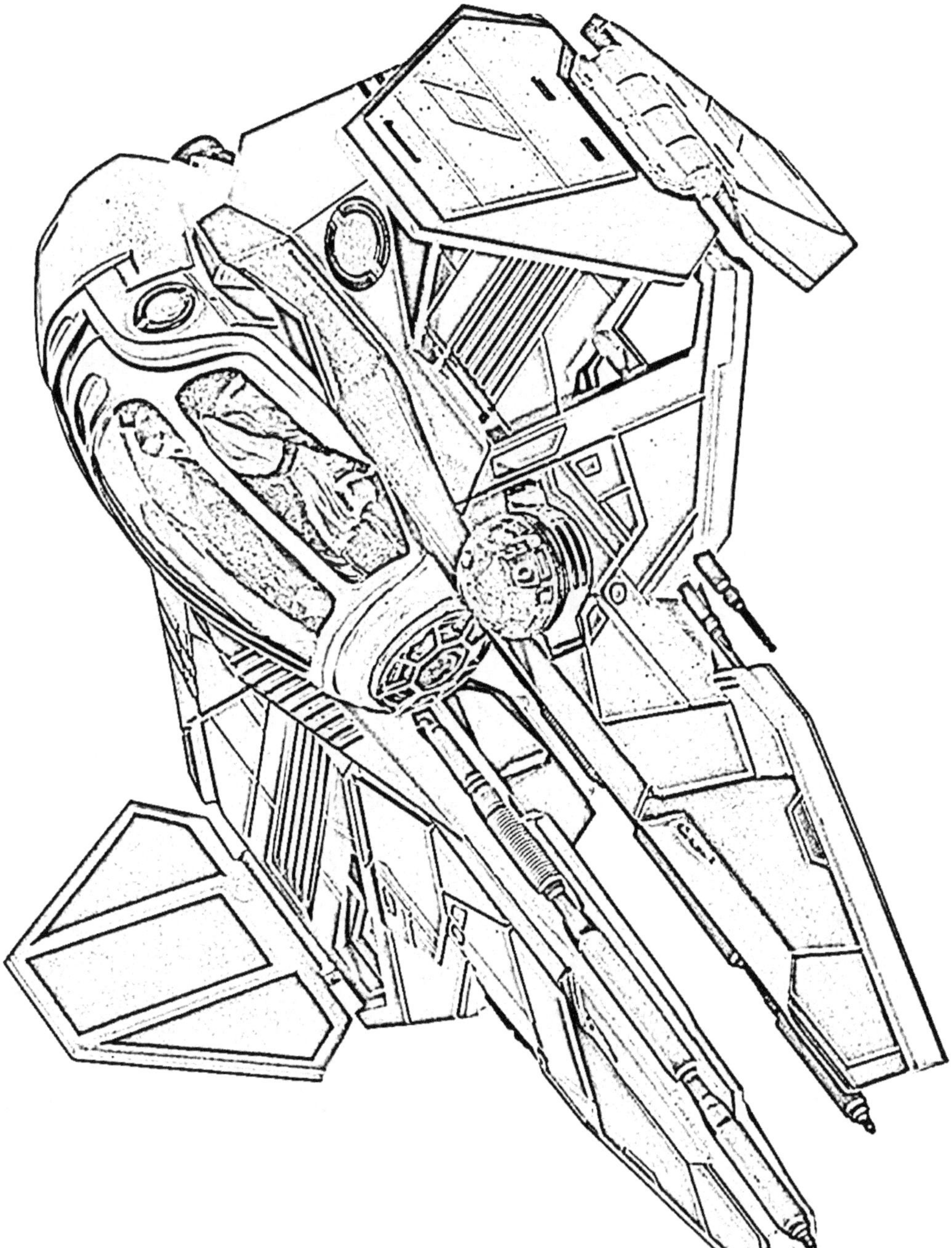

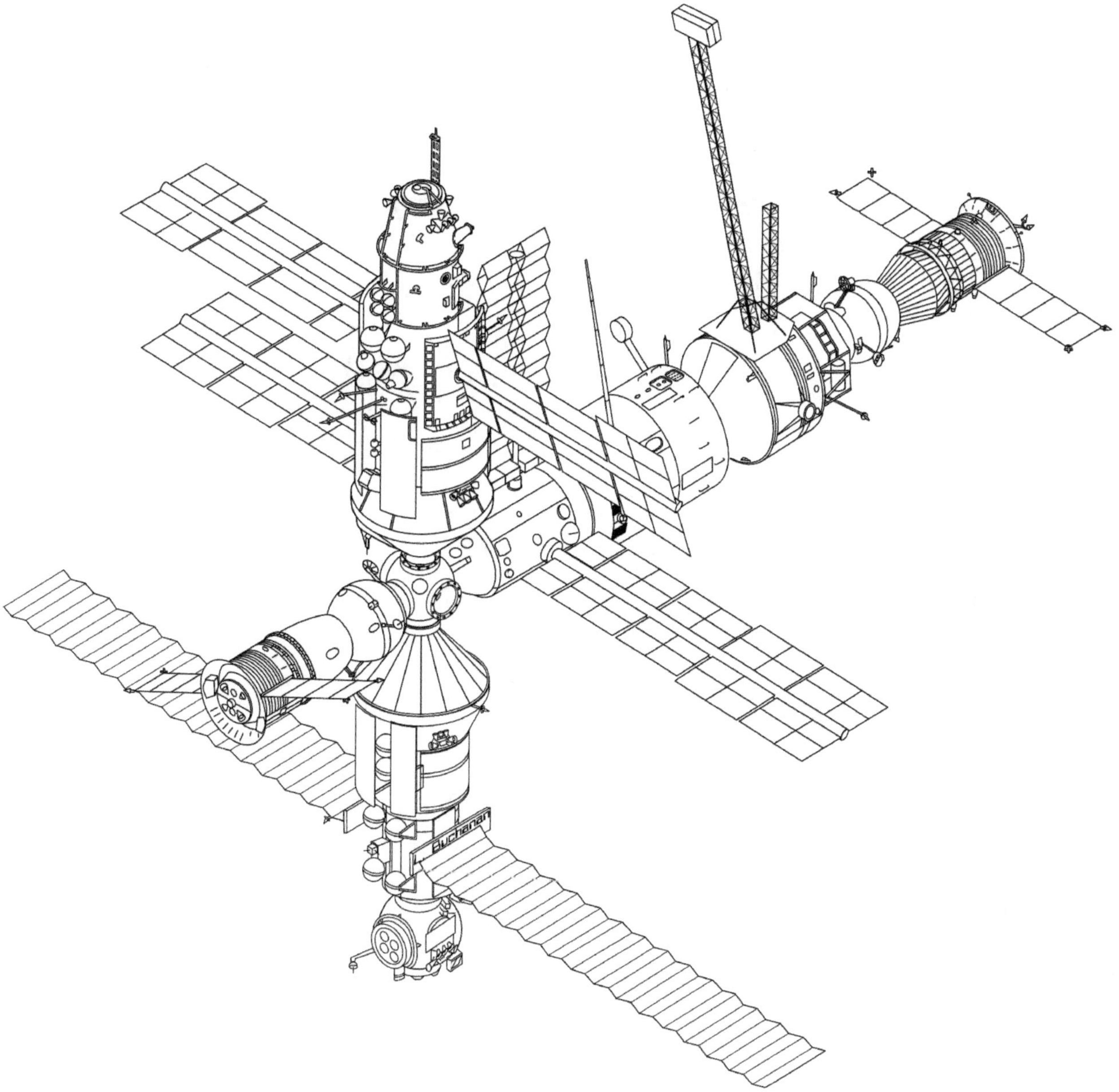
Buchanan

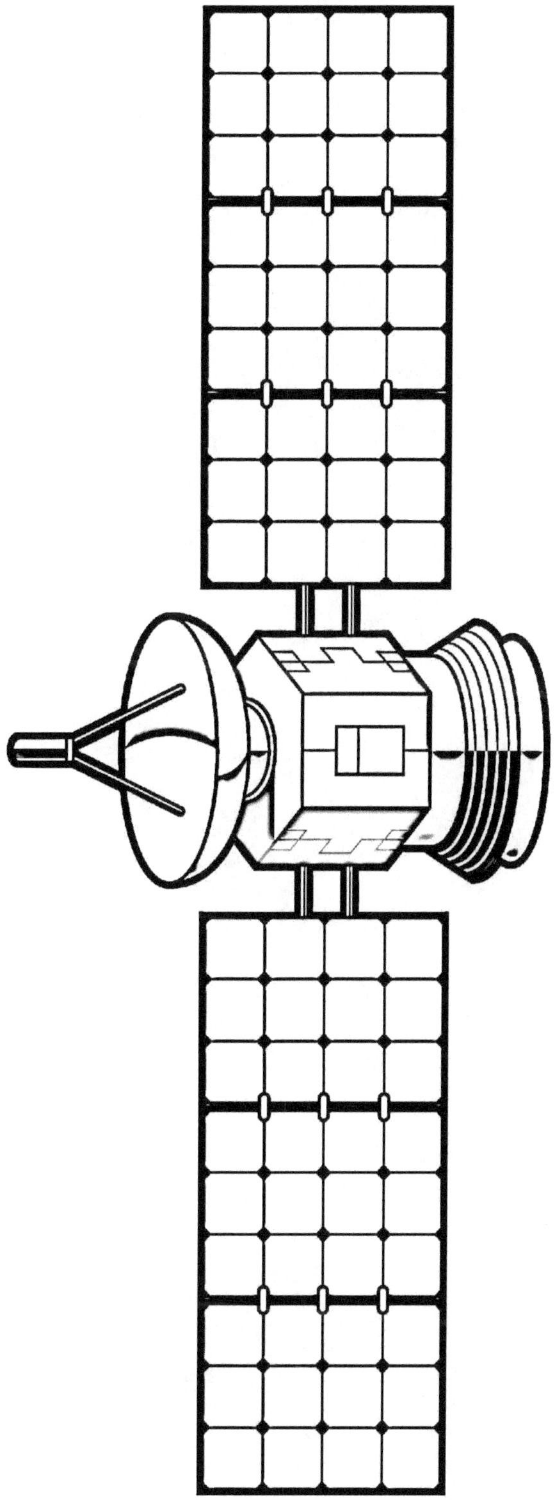

CPSIA information can be obtained
at www.ICGtesting.com
Printed in the USA
LVHW102140310320
651834LV00006B/189

9 781973 484684